Title

ESCAI

First published by the Ashford Writers in 1994

Copyright 1994 'The Ashford Writers'

Copyright is retained by the individual subscribers

Cover design and Illustrations

Pat McNeill

Compilation, word processing and preparation
for publication by
Marjorie Burge - Freda Evans - Tom Wilson
Lori Reich - Pat McNeill

Hubert Moore, who guides Ashford Writers, is the author of : 'Down by a Bicycle' 'Namesakes' 'Rolling Stock'

Previous anthologies published by Ashford Writers
'Mirages' and 'Wings'

Our grateful thanks to
Ashford Federation of the Arts
Keith Rundell and Ian Shoebridge of Ashford Library

No part of this production may be reproduced, stored in a retrieval system or transmitted in any form or by any means, electronic, mechanical, photocopying, recording or otherwise without the permission of the subscribers concerned

PREFACE

To escape can in some circumstances be an act of courage which most of us wouldn't attempt. In terms of writing it doesn't seem at all courageous. Isn't it after all what writing is about – closing the door on reality and safely creating for ourselves another world, a world of marvellous warmth or of fantastic excitement? Certainly on the first Tuesday evening of the month (Ashford Writers' regular meeting time), the Library is locked off from the real world of pub and police station and is a haven of peace interrupted only by the occasional thud through the front door of returning videos.

Perhaps, however, the title of this selection of recent work should be followed by an exclamation mark. The opening line of the first item in the selection – "Waggons Roll!" by Marjorie Burge – reads 'Ashford is being pedestrianised' – a laudable act maybe, but hardly the language of escapism. The second item challenges our expectations more openly: what sort of escape is this, if we are to find ourselves in the collapsed and all–too–real world of Barbara Brant Smiths' "Cardboard City"?

Item four is the title-story of the selection, Kay Schlapp's "Escape". Here again there is no sense of euphoria, no avoidance of the real world. There's "an odd lightness", a moment suddenly "empty of tears", but nothing is easy, escape is "up the hill" rather than down, a realisation of positive feeling rising to the surface despite what's called later in the selection "the skin of despair".

Escape, it seems, is the opposite of escapism. To judge by the writing here, it entails facing reality, refusing to settle for the safety of a make–believe world, saying sadly but realistically "Farewell, Andalusia". There's despair, of course; but there's also a delicately–handled delight: in the words of one of Letitia Hughes' fine poems, "The Spirit of Glasgow NW", '...that very morning/that love had left him/was the morning that the girl walked/ (not floating) in the sun...'.

Not floating but walking.

Hubert Moore

CONTENTS

WAGGONS ROLL! (Marjorie Burge)	1
CARDBOARD CITY (Barbara Brant Smith)	2
LOST LOVE (Marjorie Burge)	3
WE WENT THERE (Letitia Hughes)	4
ESCAPE (Kay Schlapp)	5
THE PRICE OF A TEAR (Colin Roberts)	7
WHERE DID MY JOB GO? (Brian Donnelly)	9
FOR DAVID CUE (Marjorie Burge)	11
I SUPPOSE (Letitia Hughes)	12
A FISHY TALE (Jean Sinclair-Hill)	13
FAREWELL, ANDALUSIA (Barbara Brant Smith)	16
BALLAD OF A BAGHDAD CHRISTMAS (Tom Wilson)	19
A BYTE TOO FAR (Tom Gooding)	21
BONDED (Pat McNeill)	26
LOOKING UP FROM UNDER A HOLM OAK (Pat McNeill)	26
SWEET AND SOUR (Letitia Hughes)	26
THE TRAIN (Jean Sinclair-Hill)	27
MARILYN (Letitia Hughes)	31
DEAD LATIN (Letitia Hughes)	32
MISTER SHUFFLEBOTHAM (Tom Wilson)	33
THE SPIRIT OF GLASGOW NW (Letitia Hughes)	37
BODDOM VOE (Colin Roberts)	38
BENNIE, SECOND TO NONE (Lori Reich)	40
FALLEN SWIFT, ASHFORD (Pat McNeill)	45
SOMETIMES, IN THE MORNING (Letitia Hughes)	46
WAVING TO STRANGERS (Marjorie Burge)	47
IN THANKS FOR JOCELYN'S POTTERY (Pat McNeill)	51
WINTER ORCHARDS SEEN FROM A TRAIN (Pat McNeill)	51
THE FACELESS SQUARE (Freda Evans)	52
THE TRAMP'S SONG (Violet Simes)	58
THE GREEN TICKET (Colin Roberts)	59

WAGGONS ROLL!

Ashford is being pedestrianised
The traffic is being diverted
And when you come to Ashford
You will find it can only be skirted.
The roads are covered in paving slabs,
Footpaths and walkways abound,
So if you've come in a motor
I'm afraid you'll have to go round.
It will be like a fort in a Western
With the townsfolk marooned inside
And the howls of encircling drivers
Will sound like an Indian tribe.
I am sure there are some who will like it
I personally think it a pity;
Perhaps we should change the name of the town
And call ourselves Dodge City.

Marjorie Burge

CARDBOARD CITY

FEW SPARED time to glance into the shadows of the recess, where Joe had made his home. A biting wind sent litter swirling down the Strand as the early evening crowds hurried towards the neon-lit theatres and the myriad restaurants of Pleasure City. They would not mar their evening's pleasure with thoughts of vagrants sleeping rough.

Alcohol was Joe's constant companion. He stared vacantly at the passersby: his drinking distanced him from the mainstream of London city life. Yet his befuddled brain knew his paltry possessions must be spread out early to stake his claim to a doorway, or the pitch would go. His cardboard boxes lay flattened on the floor, ready to assemble for the night. A last bout of spirits would, with luck, anaesthetise him in this thin cocoon against the cold in the small hours before the dawn.

Joe put his hands into his pockets to catch whatever warmth seeped from his frail body. If he got too chilled before nightfall, sleep came in fits and starts. And if the night grew bitter, it could turn into the big sleep from which he would not wake.

His disordered mind had severed the memories of childhood, when loving parents had cushioned their simple son from the vagaries of life. Their death in Joe's early manhood had sent him out to battle with the world. His only sanctuary became a lodging house for rootless men.

Joe's fingers fumbled with his wallet, a remainder from more prosperous days when oddjob painting earned a little money. His thoughts rambled over times past at the hostel: its beds in curtained cubicles, men to sit beside at meals.

The hostel closed. Uneconomic, the authorities had said. Joe's world collapsed. The inmates drifted on their separate ways and Joe, without the lifeline of an institution, spiralled downwards into a world of alcohol and survival on the streets.

A clock struck nine. The Salvation Army lady had not combed the alleyways that evening with her message of salvation and a mug of soup. To appease the hunger nagging in his stomach, he might as well bed down.

Discarded sheets of newspaper, harvested from the bins of lamp posts, stuffed his tattered coat and trousers. His cloth cap was pulled well down. Joe slowly wound a treasured length of twine around his waist to bind his clothes more tightly. Then, with a quick gulp from a bottle, like a hibernating animal he crept into his box to seek oblivion.

Another day of makeshift living in the great metropolis was over.

Barbara Brant Smith

LOST LOVE

A gradual process,
unlike the setting of the sun
which merely dips from sight
allows the world to turn,
silent as sleep,
and reappears.

No real warning;
cloud-obscured, smoke-screened,
soft-footed, chameleon,
slips from the hand and heart,
silent as star dust
and disappears.

Marjorie Burge

We went there
And Lily was gone.
Her view of the world
Through aspidistra-cloaked windows
In the green half light
Of a dry Sunday
In a damp-pervaded room;
Where the bricks, hammered in
To make the floor
Were covered by carpet worn down
By visiting.
Childhoods children, now older,
Remember her, and the damp
That is only recalled on reflection;
Remember instead the sunlight dust
Through the door leading back,
And everlasting smells of buns and bacon.
And her view of the world, green,
Before they took it away,
Took it and shaped it into something
New, and undamp as a bank manager's eye;
Lived in not by love, but by design.
Then they knocked it down (for a price),
And all the Lilies of the world
Went with it.

Letitia Hughes

ESCAPE

HER HEART was leaping, the blood sang in her ears, and she gasped again and again for breath. All she could see was the patch of short grass by the hawthorn hedge, lit gold by the evening sun. Gratefully she stumbled towards it and almost fell to the ground. Sheer fury had driven her up the hill to this well-known place where she had often rested.

Little by little her breathing slowed, and she began to be aware of the quietness around her. She began to be aware also of an ache in her ribs and a tenderness on the left side of her face, and as she let these small pains surface, so the larger pain which was the thought of him returned. Slowly she began to weep, her fury seeping out in incomprehending despair.

It had all started so wonderfully - he was such fun to be with, made everyone laugh. He had bought her flowers, told her she was the only girl for him, kissed her and made love to her as she had believed possible only in her fantasies. She had been swept off her feet, and they had set up house together in spite of the doubts of some of her friends and relations. Now everything had turned to ashes. He seemed to have changed; sometimes a terrifying second self emerged. She could never tell when it would happen - there seemed to be no pattern. He would pick an argument, and no matter how calm and reasonable she tried to be, it would always escalate into a shouting match, and then he would start hitting her. The first few times she had been incredulous, and he had been contrite and promised never, ever, to do it again. She had bought a makeup stick to hide her black eyes, and always wore her glasses in public.

It wasn't just the hitting. He called her names as well - bitch, whore - these were the most frequent. He said she never listened to him, that she wasn't a real person, that she didn't love him. He tore up some of her dresses. After these scenes there was always a silence from him, a dreadful walled-in silence, lasting sometimes for a couple of days. She had tried with heart, soul and body to show she loved him, hoping that with patience she could have helped him, but her effort was futile. This evening it had all happened again, and afterwards she had managed to escape up the hill.

Hugging her knees, she sat, at last empty of tears, gazing aimlessly at the little insects creeping about in the grass, while the rosy light of the setting sun warmed her tired being. All at once she realised clearly that this time it was different - this time it was finished. She had come to the end of what she had to give him - there was nothing left. It was so obvious that she wondered why she had not thought of it before. Tomorrow she would pack her bags and leave while he was at work.

When the shadows slid across the grass to where she was sitting, she got up with an odd lightness in her heart, and set off for the place called "home". The old familiar path down the hill had never before seemed so beautiful.

Kay Schlapp

THE PRICE OF A TEAR

Admission the price of a tear
through a fence of passing legs.
On a mirror wet floor
with a cardboard door
and hands all wrapped in rags.

You won't see if you don't look
at the fingers that peep from the sleeves;
At the crumpled cans
that hang from the hands
of a tramp who is still in his teens.

The city he knows
is a forest of hose,
and neon that shines in the gutter,
wears alligator shoes
for rutting and booze,
that cares not a damn for his stutter.

You won't see if you don't look
down at the eyes looking up.
Through the railings of legs,
these are the dregs,
stuck in a cardboard cup.

Suffused like the damp
from his pavement camp,
his blood chills at the thought of eviction.
For the sewer nearby
keeps his slabs dry,
and his new mate has no sort of addiction.

*He's one of the one's
living off crumbs,
thrown down out of some kind of pity.
His main sin, you see,
is he's one short in three,
that's common in cardboard city.*

*So if you've a mind,
and dare look behind,
as you step smartly by in distaste,
they are vagrants maybe,
but the truth is, you see,
They all need your time not your haste.*

Colin Roberts

WHERE DID MY JOB GO?

JOHN RETURNED to work from holiday, feeling anything but refreshed; in fact as he tramped through reception and up the stairs to his office on the first floor, he felt the normal Monday morning feeling, only a thousand times worse. He realised he needed another holiday when he passed his boss on the way, getting no response at all to his at least half enthusiastic "Good morning".

As he pushed open the double doors to the office, he felt a strange, almost wild-west type atmosphere hit him as he received a combination of eye contact avoidance, guilty half smiles and complete silence. What a greeting, he thought, wishing he was still lazing by the pool in brilliant sunshine. As John looked around, he realised something else was not quite right. By the time his eyes had drunk in the full vista of his bureaucratic environment, it had sunk in that something was missing. His job had disappeared.

He immediately tried to engage various of his colleagues in a short question and answer routine but was told by each of them that they were too busy, and that he would have to look for his job himself. He had read in the paper before about jobs disappearing, especially while people were on holiday, but he'd never imagined it could happen to him. His mind revisited the eve of his last day before his holiday, when his boss told him to enjoy himself with a sincerity that had seemed totally alien to him.

At length he did manage to get one of the less hostile people in the office to talk to him.

"I'm sorry John but I haven't seen it at all. Where did you leave it?"

"Well, it was just here, between you and Mrs Wood before I went away."

"Well it can't have gone far. Has anyone seen John's job?" he shouted across an indifferent office.

The response was patchy, to say the least. A few people looked in their desks, under their desks, in their waste paper bins, but no one could find it. John, who was never very good with figurative language, decided to take the bull between his teeth and gallop, wailing and gnashing, into the sunset of his boss's office. There was only one problem, his boss wasn't there. He thought he would build up the pressure on him by waiting there, pacing up and down until here returned. When he did, John got straight to the point.

"My job has disappeared."
"Yes, you're right."
"Oh, you know."
"Yes, it was me who disappeared it!"
"Well, where is it?"
"I'm afraid it's lost forever."
"So, what do I do now?"
"Go and look for another one - somewhere else."

This last remark was accompanied by both a smug grin and a brown envelope. John looked around in this pokey office, anything to avoid looking at his boss. In a strange way this helped him, momentarily, to avoid the issue at hand. As he gazed around, he saw, on the large board behind his boss's head, a list, ostensibly of tasks his boss had to accomplish. The first said simply "John's job to go". It was then that he realised of course that the writing was on the wall.

He took the envelope before the offer was withdrawn and trudged out through the silent but busy office towards the stairs from whence he came.

No tears were shed for him, but why should they be?

Brian Donnelly

*FOR DAVID CUE - WHO CYCLES PAST ME WHILST I WALK
BOTH OF US NAVIGATING HYTHE ROAD ON OUR WAY TO WORK*

*Wheels skimming the surface
he goes surf riding by
while I wave from the
safety of the shore
his greeting
thrown into the wind
reaches my ears
and my 'hi David'
tugs his head half circle
his one visible eye
gleaming wickedly
his face alive
with exhilaration
and then he's away
dipping and rising
with the swell
riding the crest
coasting past islands
easing round the mainland
into the dockyard
and leg over bowsprit,
land lubbered,
anchored down for the day,
giving his crew hell,
he waits for the tide
when once more he's
into the slipstream
eyeing the maelstrom
setting his compass
driving towards the Pole
racing the Cape
on his two-wheeled schooner.*

Marjorie Burge

I suppose
You know it is.
I suppose this
from.....
And I suppose
As another day dawns,
supposing that
my soul, broken,
and placed upon your tongue,
delivers you divine
into the chanting world,
blessed with love
and secret ritual.
In the seven day Sunday
which is yours,
do you glow?
Or is it a trick
Of the light.

Letitia Hughes

A FISHY TALE

THERE WAS an unearthly crash and I awoke with a start. I thought I must be dreaming, for through a gaping hole in the ceiling nose-dived a shark.

We lived miles from the sea, that was my first thought and my second thought was, My God they actually eat people! He slithered to a stop at the end of my bed and pulling the duvet around me I grabbed the phone on the bedside table and dialled 999. I felt unreal as I listened to the buzz, buzz on the line at the other end, and I still felt unsure if this was reality or if I was having some sort of nightmare. A voice broke into my thoughts asking if I required assistance from the Police, Ambulance or Fire Brigade. I collected my thoughts quickly, and decided that I needed some kind of miracle and asked if I could be put through to the top man.

The voice at the other end repeated the words - Police, Fire or Ambulance - and I said "Neither, put me through on the hot line to God".

It seemed like an eternity before I head a deep voice proclaim "This is Heaven calling, can I help you?"

The relief showed in my voice as I answered "Oh, is that God?"

The dark brown voice answered "No madam, I am the lodge keeper at the golden gates. Which department do you require?"

I thought a second before I replied.

"I suppose it would be the lost property department, because I wondered if you had mislaid a shark. I've just had one fall out of the heavens, through my ceiling onto my bedroom floor, and by now he's looking in a very sorry state, as he needs water and there's no way I can get him into my bath. Anyway he might eat me if I get too near to him."

"Just a minute Miss" said the gate keeper, "I think I had better put you through to Head Office. Hang on a moment."

As I waited, I listened to the recorded celestial music of harp playing, and then a silvery voice said "This is Angel. God's personal Secretary. What seems to be the problem?" I repeated to her my predicament and she said "Oh dear, just a moment, I'll see if God can have a word with you." I could hear a whispered conversation, and then a man's voice, smooth as honey, soft as silk, said "Hello my dear, I believe you must be the lady who has been chosen to help to feed the five thousand. Don't worry, it's all being taken care of." There was a click as his phone was replaced, and before I had time to collect my wits about me, there was a blinding flash and a lot of smoke.

Scared witless, I pulled the duvet up over my head, and when I plucked up enough courage to peep out I was relieved to see that the shark had disappeared but every vacant space in my bedroom was filled with packets of fish fingers! "My God," I thought, "I must have gone mad, I must be hallucinating, I shouldn't have drunk that half bottle of red wine last night. I shall be suffering from the DT's, I shall be seeing pink elephants and little green men next."

I jumped when the phone rang again and I gazed at it transfixed, unable to pluck up the courage to pick it up, but the ringing persisted, and I gingerly lifted up the receiver and gave my number. A man's voice answered and said "We've received notification that you have in your possession a consignment of fishfingers." I said in a quavering voice, "It appears so." He said, "Well, love, we need them up here at the Town Hall - we've already got the loaves. We've got five thousand homeless people to feed and they are all starving. I'll be sending round some transport to pick them upright away."

Click went the phone as he hung up before I had time to ask any questions. My God! I thought, I'd better put something on - I was only wearing a shortie nightie, and I grabbed my dressing-gown that was hanging over the end of the bed. No question of getting dressed, my wardrobe doors were blocked by packets of fishfingers stacked up against them.

I pulled back the bedroom curtains and peered out at the early morning, wondering vaguely what the weather was like. I was staggered to see a piano go past the window followed by a couple of armchairs so I opened the casement to get a better look. There was water lapping round the window sill and it finally penetrated into my addled brain that I was in the middle of a flood.

Then I heard a voice say "Ahoy there" and looking to my left I saw a barge of some size making its way towards me. It slithered to stop as it drew level with my window and a bearded man wearing a naval peaked cap informed me that they had come to collect the consignment of fishfingers. Whereupon two men wearing wetsuits waded up to the window. One pushed past me and climbed into my bedroom and started the seemingly endless task of transferring the contents onto the barge via his wetsuited friend standing halfway between.

"You could help us love" he said, tossing a packet of dustbin bags at me.

"Just a minute," I exclaimed, "I want to know what's going on. Where did all that water come from out there?"

"Well Miss," he replied, "it seems there has been some sort of upheaval at sea which has caused a series of great tidal waves, and the river has burst its banks and flooded the whole area. It's lucky for you that you live on high ground, the people down in the valley have been sitting on their roofs all night and they are cold and starving. It seems that some guy called Canute is being sent in to command the water to be sent back to where it came from."

Nice chap he was - I could see he fancied me but somehow I thought there was something fishy about him. Oh well! I thought, I might as well be hung for a sheep as a lamb and got back in bed with what was left of the bottle of red wine. I must have dozed off, for when I woke up the sun was streaming in the window and there was no sign of any water outside. The bloke Canute must have been good at his job I thought, and then I thought about the nice chap in the wetsuit and was motivated to get up and tart myself up. I went up to the Town Hall and hung about to see if I could catch sight of him. I go up there most days now but I've never bumped into him yet. Funny thing! But when I try to talk to people about the flood, they just give me a funny look and hurry away.

Anyone would think I'd dreamt it all - well you never know, maybe I did.

Jean Sinclair-Hill

FAREWELL, ANDALUSIA

AH! ANDALUSIA! That was where in middle age my love affair with the white villages of the sierras began.

The little pueblo house of uncut stone, plastered and whitened under its red pantile roof, was mine and it was moving day.

The Guardia Civil with his hooded watchful eyes sat idly on a chair by the barracks at the entrance to the pueblo, noting my vanload of possessions.

I was aware of another onlooker, as I crossed my threshold: a swarthy youth in black shirt and rough black trousers, who had pulled a chair onto the pavement and, unabashed, was monitoring my every move. His face, coarsened by long hours of toil in the campo, was set with piercing eyes, shaded from the fierce heat by a beret.

I had hoped that while the pueblo slumbered in the mid-day heat, I could ease myself into village life unnoticed, but a stranger is news in the sierras and a circle of black clad women soon joined the seated youth. As each article of furniture was lifted from the van, a swell of whispers rose and fell. "That's her dead husband!" I heard one murmur as I proudly carried my bust of Napoleon to its new niche inside my home. It was a relief to escape into the dark interior of the house.

Early next morning I pushed open the shutters and stood entranced at the tumbled roofscape of red pantiles. Straggling rows of cube-like houses ran between the Moorish castle and a deserted convent, where kestrels bred. And there in the cobbled street was the Spaniard, waiting at my door.

"Yo Francisco" he said, proffering me his roughened hand. I guessed from his gesticulation that we were neighbours. He lived in the next-door casita, where he stalled his mule in a basement stable.

Out of the goodnature of his heart, and with the simple curiosity of the peasant about a stranger, Francisco initiated me into the ways of village life. He accompanied me to the market where peasants hoped to earn a few pesetas with meagre offerings of spinach, ragged bunches of carrots, earthy potatoes and sprigs of mountain herbs.

To me a major hurdle was tracking down the shops hidden behind their wooden persian blinds. Darkened living rooms concealed haphazard mounds of tinned goods, alcohol and hardware. Francisco proudly introduced me to Maraquita, one of the village women whose commercial prowess had funded a garish three piece suite, which entirely overwhelmed her little house.

Women gossiped at the wash-house, as they pounded out their linen in cold water, before strewing it on wayside boulders to bleach in the morning sun. They chaffed Francisco on his self-appointed task as chaperone. The dustcart's claxon sounded and hordes of hungry cats darted out from doorways waiting for the refuse scraps which might fall upon the ground.

My debt to Francisco deepened as the months went by. He became the son I had never had. Village tradition and customs had circumscribed his life. He could not read or write. But, he perceived the changing patterns of light upon the mountains, the fiery sunsets and the lights of Africa twinkling on the far horizon under a night-sky full of stars.

His love of the countryside was passionate. We walked in groves of olives where golden orioles and bee-eaters flitted among the branches. We climbed the criss-cross mule tracks on the mountains to the tinkling bells of goats. Then we would rest beneath the wild limestone crags to watch the vultures on the rising thermals floating free in a cloudless azure sky. In the wooded valley near Manilva the limpid pools, where Roman Tiberius had bathed, teemed with trout and terrapin. The woods of Algotocin were carpeted with white spring bulbs.

One evening over coffee Francisco told me of his father's youth. How he had poached for rabbits to keep his family from hunger; his grinding labour in the cork forests stripping bark, urged on by an overseer armed with a raw-hide whip. Long festering grievances were settled in the Civil War, when Communists lined up the local landowners in one of the pueblo's squares to be summarily shot.

One day this idyllic life was shattered. A letter from England demanded my return to settle family matters. I had to go, so with a heavy heart I locked my village house and gave Francisco the key.

I little knew that it would be two years before I returned to the sierras, although I often haunted their byways in my dreams.

At last the time came when I turned the corner in the Barrio Alto to see the panorama past Gibraltar to the distant purple ranges of the Atlas. It still had the power to hold me spellbound. But the ham factory now was silent; the olive press was still. The knot of old men in ancient suits and berets no longer gathered near the cafe to pass the time of day. The panniered donkeys which climbed the alleys had vanished. A stream of pop-music blared from open doorways.

I sensed bad news. Maria, shelling beans on the doorstep, exclaimed to see me and ran inside to fetch my key. Where was Francisco, my anchor in the village? She told me of an accident in the campo that had killed him earlier in the year.

The spell was broken. I knew new values had eaten into my beloved pueblo. My sojourn there was at an end. I climbed the hill up to the barracks and turned to pay a last adieu to the white-washed village set among its crags. I remembered the day of my arrival and the youth, who had scanned my movements with his intense probing eyes.

Farewell, Francisco! Your fiery love of Andalusia enriched my life.

Barbara Brant Smith

BALLAD OF A BAGHDAD CHRISTMAS

Beside the Tigris' muddy banks
By High Command forgot,
Two Hundred British Other Ranks
Were dumped and left to rot.
To fields in barren countryside
In Army trucks we rode
A tented hospital to building
Along the Washash Road.

At nightfall we returned to Camp
And dreary dull routine
Playing pontoon by lantern light
In the noisy men's canteen.
The seniors in the Sergeants' Mess
Had seen it all before;
Long-service 'regulars', one and all,
Promoted in the War.

From shipyards and colliery towns
They had been glad to roam.
The Army gave them security
They could not find at home.
Amongst them, fresh from grammar school,
Were young technicians who
Came from nice suburban streets
To a world both coarse and new.

For Christmas Day, the Mess was planning
A dinner to prepare
With turkey, spuds and brussels sprouts
And Scotch and beer to spare.
Each Sergeant would contribute
Ten dinars from his pay,
So that the Sergeant Major's mates
Could make the season gay.

One volunteer was needed (though
It did seem rather hard)
To stay Out There on Christmas Day
And mount the picket guard.
So then I said, "I wouldn't mind
And I will volunteer.
I don't care for turkey or stuffing,
Someone else can drink my beer."

Oh, it was quiet and peaceful there
Out on that barren site;
Stars in a cloudless sky above
The velvet desert night.
The picket's meal was meagre, spare,
Tinned vegetable stew with beef.
The time passed slowly till the dawn
Arrived with our relief.

My mates said, "Weren't you lucky Tug!
You've had a quiet night.
Our dinner was a washout and
We nearly had a fight.
Some idiot let the cooks get drunk;
They set the tent ablaze.
We put it out but the grub was spoiled-
So much for Christmas Days!"

Tom Wilson

A BYTE TOO FAR

BAKER LOOKED at each of them in turn, making no attempt to hide his dismay.

"Now then Morgan, you say that this morning it was running perfectly."

"Yes sir, Mr Baker, I logged in and it greeted me with the usual goodmorning and asked me how my weekend had gone."

"Usual greeting you say; was it usual for it to greet you in such an informal manner?"

Baker had walked around the table and was standing behind the younger man.

"Well, it was for me, sir," he replied, his eyes locked steadfastly upon the table top. "It addressed us all differently. It was more formal when talking to Dr Hewit or Dr Parker."

"Hm, yes . . ." Baker paused, deliberately putting pressure on Morgan, who, his face colouring, could only wonder at why he was being picked on and feared that Baker might already know the truth. "You make it sound as though it had a mind of its own, lad," Baker continued, moving closer, sensing Morgan's discomfort and ready to exploit a weak link.

"Leave him alone, Jack, the program was doing exactly what it was designed to do, that is react intelligently with humans in real time."

Jennifer Parker looked tired. She was nervously toying with a Biro, twiddling it through her fingers.

"So then, Dr Parker," Baker regarded the woman bleakly irritated by her interruption. "Perhaps you can tell us why the most powerful computer money can buy, running the world's finest AI programme, crashed, wiping clean not only its data files but its memory as well and all within hours of the world's press descending on us."

"If we knew that, Baker, we might have it running now, we wouldn't be wasting valuable time finding a scapegoat." Clive Hewit slouched in his seat looking thoroughly hacked off. A small man, he did not suffer fools gladly, which made life somewhat of a misery for him because by his standards the world was populated by fools, and at this moment Jack Baker was up there with government ministers, economists and most of his fellow scientists.

'Don't you dare preach to me about time," Baker rounded on Hewit, his self control slipping. "The time and, might I add, money that we have spent on this project could have sent a man to Mars and very probably brought him back again. And now within a single morning, you have, between the three of you, managed to lose the whole damn thing."

"We didn't lose anything Jack, it just crashed," Jenny Parker chipped in attempting to calm the situation. "You know that we are operating at the very limits of computing technology. There was always an outside chance that this might happen. By pushing on too fast, all we achieved was to shorten the odds on suffering a breakdown."

Baker stepped back from the lad and with a measured step and a calculated silence returned to his seat at the end of the table.

"Suffered a breakdown," he echoed softly, a dry sarcastic laugh chasing his words, "Suffered a breakdown. Jesus wept, woman." He bellowed as though trying to pin her to her chair with his voice. "It's a machine just like your Hotpoint. Machines don't suffer breakdowns, people break them."

Hewit had been watching Baker, with the detached disdain that he normally reserved for obsequious waiters at over priced restaurants.

"But this wasn't just a machine, was it, Baker?" he cut in before Dr Parker could recover from Baker's onslaught. "It had a capacity for real intelligence and was capable of independent thought, the work it was doing on tunnelling electrons was invaluable, and it was doing this work without any input from Dr Parker or myself, but you wanted to do publicity stunts for journalists."

"Oh, I see, so it's my fault," Baker rounded on Hewit, his words mocking. "The government pays the likes of Dr Parker and yourself astronomical salaries and when you can't bring home the bacon, suddenly I'm to blame."

"No one else here wanted to give it human characteristics, Baker." Hewit had quit his indolent slough and was sitting upright in his seat meeting Baker eye to eye. "It was you who wanted it to be able to converse with laymen journalists and swop inane banter with politicians' wives."

"And how else do you think we would have got the funding Hewit? The average politician would not know a tunnelling electron if it imbedded itself in his skull and sung three choruses of Dixie."

"We could have got the funding by getting results, Jack" Dr Parker said, flashing a warning glance across at Hewit with a shake of her head, "Barry Morgan has spent the last eight months feeding the machine information about the world outside and making conversation with it. The time would have been better spent on more subtle research. Look, whilst it was soaking up all that Barry was giving it, it was simultaneously working on both my and Dr Hewit's projects, as well as doing random work of its own. The most galling thing is we do not understand how it managed to do it."

"So what you are saying, Dr Parker, is that the machine was out of control, running unsupervised data and programmes."

"No it was not running unsupervised, Baker," Hewit cut in, incensed by what he perceived to be a slur on his professional credibility. "The machine was intelligent. I appreciate that you might find the concept hard to grasp, but intelligence implies independent thoughts and emotions."

'Emotions, Dr Hewit? How can a machine have emotions? Your brief was to design and produce a computer capable of demonstrating Artificial Intelligence, not emotions. Ants have intelligence, they don't need or possess emotion, neither does a computer."

"Insects do not possess intelligence, Baker," Hewit retorted, as though talking to a child. "They are instinctive. What we tried to produce here was an alien intelligence, more ape than ant but with a learning and memory capability greater than ours. But you wanted it to mirror human intelligence, that is what we did and that is what probably destroyed it."

"N-no, that's what definitely destroyed it, Mr Baker," Barry Morgan was surprised to hear his own voice in what was all of a sudden a very lonely and large office. "You see, it became quite attached to me over the months that I have spent with it. This morning I told it about my forthcoming wedding and the home that we are buying up country. I hadn't told it about my life outside before and I think it came as a shock to it. Any way I told it that there would be someone else along to talk to it and it went sort of quiet like it was sulking. It had done that before but in the past it just carried on with some other problem. This time it just shut down. It wasn't until Dr Parker tried to access it that we realised that it had gone for good."

"Now then let's get this straight." Baker was having trouble taking on board what Morgan had just said. "Are you trying to tell me that the machine died of a broken heart?"

"That's about the gist of it, Jack" Jennifer Parker confirmed "You see it was lonely, we had given it a powerful intellect and then let it exist in its own dark world without love or companionship. It could not face the prospect of Barry leaving so it just let go."

Baker finally snapped, turning on the woman. "Are you telling me that the machine was in love with the boy? Well?" Dr Parker flinched before Baker's tirade. "That this, this monster that you created was a damn faggot?"

The words hit her like a slap in the face, the Biro that she had been toying with snapped into three bits, the centre section bouncing off the far wall and her chair falling back as she jumped to her feet.

"How dare you!" she said, all self control lost. "Of all the arrogant. . . How dare you assume that the machine had a male personality! I programmed the human characteristics that you so desperately wanted. I created its persona. Part of me went into that machine. It was more female than you will ever be a man." She paused, breathing deeply. "All you had to do," she said, her voice dropping to muted tones that thinly veiled her anger, "Was stand up to the politicians and let us do what we are paid to do. But no, you had to pander to their whims and now we are right back..."

A knock at the door cut Dr Parker short, the door swung open and a head bobbed around the corner. "The gentlemen of the press are here, Sir, shall I send them up?"

Baker sat down, his head in his hands, the grey drape of defeat blanketing the room. Silently the others gathered their notes and left the office, leaving Baker to the wolves.

Tony Gooding

BONDED

Sad as flags in rain
Sweet as may in bloom
Warm as mother's lap
Fierce as frost on pane
Dark as yew tree's gloom
Hurt as fox in trap

Hoarse as she I cry
Born for joy and lust
Doomed to thee am I
Love but thee I must   Pat McNeill

LOOKING UP FROM UNDER A HOLM OAK

Frayed and fretted scraps of heaven's brightness
Cotton-blue caught in the clutch of branches
Draw my eye up to find this mesh of tatters,
A prize of light. Dizzy I fall against the trunk
Gasp at the gift.

Pat McNeill

SWEET AND SOUR

We met again with the tang of sweet and sour in the air.
The bag you carried from the Chinese chippy
embarrassed you, in the light of past romantic gallantries.
Me newly married, you took your rice (special fried)
Home.
And ate up all your aspirations.

Letitia Hughes

THE TRAIN

RETURNING returning, returning, returning.

The train sang the words as it ate up the miles, and the lady sitting in the corner seat of the railway carriage, gazed with unseeing eyes at the countryside as it rushed past the window.

She tried to remember exactly how long she had been away, and recalled that she had left the country at the first ominous signs of war in the early summer of 1939, with the family who had employed her as a nursemaid to their two young children. Her thoughts dwelt on the wealthy Jewish family, and particularly on the young husband who had thought it prudent to send his wife and young family to the comparative safety of America to stay with his kinsman. She remembered that he had no doubt that war would come, for he was well informed about the dark happenings in Nazi Germany. She thought with admiration of the way he and many of his influential friends had successfully organised escape routes for German Jewish folk, and how he had vowed that he would continue to do so for as long as it was needed, and would also serve his adopted country in any way he could. She pictured again the concern on his face when he first broached the subject of evacuation to America. How he had expressed his fears about the consequences for all of them should Britain be defeated. He had explained that he felt it better to suffer the pain of parting than risk the agony of torture from the Nazis should his worst fears be realised, and went on to talk of the might of the German war machine, and of how Britain was so unprepared.

The lady in the corner seat reflected on all this as the train sped on. She thought about her life in America, of how homesick she had been in the beginning, and remembered how quickly that had passed as the American people she had met had opened their homes to her as well as their hearts, and saw herself as she was then, pretty, a typical English rose standing out from the average American girl. What fun it had all been, in constant demand for dates with all the boys she met when she was off duty. She felt again the guilt that had overcome her when war had finally enveloped her country, and the horror when she read of the suffering of her people, and of how she had counted her blessings that she was ensconced in a land of milk and honey. She remembered how worried she had been about her family back home in Devon, being the eldest of five children, three brothers and one sister, and of how she had tried to compensate for her guilt by sending home food parcels at regular intervals, hoping that they all arrived intact.

Returning, returning, returning, returning.

The train roared on echoing the thoughts that raced around in her head. She thought of the young GI whom she had eventually married soon after America had been brought into the war by the bombing of Pearl Harbour, and felt nostalgia when she relived again their impromptu wedding before he was posted overseas, of how he had desperately wanted to have her as his wife waiting for him on his return.

Returning, returning, returning, returning.

The train clattered on, and she felt her teeth bite into her lower lip as she recalled the heartbreak she had felt when she realised that he was not going to return, and that she would be left to bring up the son who had been conceived on his embarkation leave before being sent to the Pacific. She pictured the Silver Star nestling in the depths of her handbag, the medal that he had been awarded posthumously after being killed in action at the hands of the Japanese. She tried to bring to mind his face, but found that her memory of him had become misted over as the years sped relentlessly on, like the train. She groped in her handbag, feeling the desire to look at his photograph again which she kept in her wallet. She felt the memories of him come flooding back to her as she gazed at the devil-may-care face with the G.I. cap worn at a rakish angle, smiling back at her. Sighing, her thoughts turned to her only beloved son as she fingered the large oval locket hanging from the heavy gold chain round her neck and she pictured her son's photograph inside.

She had hoped that the decision she had made to make America her permanent home had been the right one, for it had seemed to her then that he would have a better chance in life in the land of his birth, but with the hindsight she now had, it seemed to her that it had been totally the wrong one, for twenty years later, he also had worn the uniform of a G.I. and was sent off to join in another bloody war in Vietnam.

Returning, returning, returning, returning.

The train rattled on relentlessly, and she felt a tear escape from each of her eyes as she thought of her son's boyish sensitive face, as he clung on to her before setting off for that alien land that was to claim his life, for he had not returned either. She recalled ruefully that there was no medal to commemorate his death, for he had not died a hero, merely as a victim of Yellow Fever. She felt more tears trickle down her face, and watched them splash on to her capacious navy blue leather handbag bought specially for the journey, and she wiped them off with her gloved hand.

Returning, returning, returning, returning.

She mentally counted up the years to the monotonous rhythm of the rocking train. She found it hard to believe that it was really twenty years ago since her son's life had been wasted in that pointless war. Groping around in her coat pocket, she found a handkerchief and blew her nose, wiping away the last of her tears. She felt amazement when she realised that she had been away from England for more than forty years. She sat up straight, sensing that the rhythm of the train was changing and that it was gradually slowing down. She felt curiosity looking out of the train window at the countryside that was revealed to her. A countryside that was adorned in all the soft tints of autumn, and she felt a pang of nostalgia as she recognised the rich brown earth of her native Devon. She heard the squeal of brakes as the train gradually ground to a halt, and feeling suddenly nervous she stood up fumbling with the handle of the carriage door, and waited hesitantly in the doorway. She felt the gentle warmth of the late afternoon sunlight as she gazed with expectant eyes at the waiting people on the station platform. She stepped down from the train as she heard the crescendo of voices, and recognised the once familiar burr of the Devon brogue. Suddenly strong arms were embracing her, ample bosoms were enveloping her, and she felt the warmth of love melting the ice that had over the years congealed around her heart.

She had come home, she had returned.

Jean Sinclair-Hill

MARILYN

2 o'clock is not
2.30
2 o'clock
is a point fixed
in space,
a mechanism for measuring
(as it turns out)
my blood pressure,
(which is rising).
The door is still shut
And music (!) is still playing
And 2 o'clock is 10 past.
I knock
You shout
I retire.
Hair spray noises (off).
Blood pressure is inversely
    proportional
to the minute hand.
It's raining outdoors.
Indoors
a storm is brewing.
I knock
You shout Oooooooo
KAYYYYYYYYYYY.
I risk opening the door.
The end of the World is nigh.
Your hair is not right . . .
You turn clockwise towards
The intruder, waiting, ready,
(ticking away).
James Dean and I stare quietly at you
doing your Marilyn impressions,
With your hair,
And tardiness.
It's 2.30.
Forget it.

Letitia Hughes

DEAD LATIN

The streets, paved with time,
Accepted us, new strata from their history.
Inconsequential now.
The smell of cooking from an English trattoria
Brings it back -
The blue heat of youth
The white glare of our uninnocence
Reflected in the stones
Where my heart still is;
And you - are you still well
And happy, though no longer
Young.
How can I imagine you
Otherwise.

Letitia Hughes

MISTER SHUFFLEBOTHAM
(This is a true story and it happened 60 years ago)

WALTER SHUFFLEBOTHAM and his wife Rosie lived together in a small Victorian house in a terrace of small Victorian houses in Hither Green, a London suburb. Walter and Rosie were both small and rotund. Since both had been born before 1900, they too were Victorian. Walter always wore a navy blue three piece suit, whatever the weather, and a grey felt hat. Rosie never left the house with out some sort of coat over her beige twinset and tweed skirt.

Ronald, their only son, when he was eighteen went off and joined the Merchant Navy. They got a postcard from him now and then with a picture of Bueonos Aires or Perth, Western Australia; but they saw very little of him any longer. On half holidays and at weekends, Walter would potter about in his small patch of garden. For their evening recreation they would link arms and toddle together down the hill to the saloon bar of 'The Duke of Clarence' where they would meet some of their cronies; respectable people like themselves who were prepared to pay a penny or twopence extra for their tipple. The Shufflebothams and their friends would never dream of mixing with the riff-raff in the Four Ale bar. Walter was the bookkeeper in a large draper's store in the Lewisham High Road, earning Four Pounds a week: so he felt he had a certain position to maintain.

Walter and Rosie both had round, cheerful faces and no strong opinions on any particular subject. So they mostly agreed with everything said by the last person who had spoken to them, which made them extremely popular among the clientele of the saloon bar. They were friendly people who liked to make friends. They were particularly fond of Molly, the vivacious dark-haired wife of Robert who was manager of the local Boots branch. Molly always made them giggle at her saucy remarks. One evening in the Duke of Clarence Molly was telling them about a droll accident.

"There I was in the greengrocer's and I trod on a wet cabbage leaf and I went arse-over-tip - Ooh, sorry! - showing all me bloomers!" The occurrence itself was so slight that it was hardly worth mentioning, but

Molly, with her sparkling eyes and gay manner put so much comical expression into her narration that poor Rosie became helpless with mirth, dabbing her streaming eyes with a scrap of pocket-handkerchief.

"Oh, Molly, what a devil you are!" she gasped. "You made me laugh so much I think I've wet myself!"

This brought a fresh burst of laughter from her friend, which was interrupted when a coarse-looking fellow in a cloth cap and shabby raincoat entered the bar and pressed some money into Molly's hand.

"Ere y'are mum" he said, " - there's three pun two and six for yer. Yer 'orse come 'ome at twelve to one. Ow! - Thank you kindly missus." Touching the broken peak of his cap, the shabby man wandered away towards the Public Bar to convert some of Molly's tip into liquid refreshment.

"Ah well," said Molly as she shoved the cash into her capacious purse, " - better be born lucky than rich, I always say. What will you have ducks?"

Walter was curious to witness this splendid shower of wealth.

"Mine's a scotch, love - Ta. Who was that bloke, Molly?" Robert shouldered his way to the bar to replenish their drinks from one of Molly's pound notes.

"Who - Tom? Oh, he sells newspapers on the corner of Lee High Road," Molly replied. "If I fancy a horse that's running I get Tom to put the money on for me."

"Doesn't that get him into trouble?" Walter was worried. "I thought street betting was against the law."

Molly gave him a broad wink. "Of course it is. It was actually Sergeant Charles of the C.I.D. who put me onto Tom. He takes bets for all the local rozzers. As long as he does it on the QT he won't ever get pinched."

Rosie was amazed. "Upon my word! - Whatever's the world coming to? My Dad never held with gambling or drink. He was strict chapel and he made my sisters and me join the Band of Hope as soon as we was eight."

Molly hooted. "So that explains why you won't ever touch anything else but ginger beer, eh, Rosie?" she challenged. Rosie simpered and emptied her glass as Robert pushed a refill of oatmeal

34

stout across the table for her.

"Oh well, - I don't really see any harm in just a little drink among friends of an evening. Only I don't have any time for men that makes a beast of themselves, like some do. And I won't stand for gambling, neither. I've seen too many homes broke up all through betting. That's one thing I can't abide. Ta, Molly - Cheers!"

As they slowly walked up the hill arm-in-arm to their terraced house, Walter could not obliterate from his mind the picture of the shabby man in his cloth cap pressing pound notes into Molly's kid-gloved hand. It happened to be the beginning of the flat racing season that week, and Walter surreptitiously began to study a copy of The Sporting Life which he had bought. The following Monday, he skipped his lunch hour and walked down Lee High Road to find Tom's newspaper stand.

That August, the temperature in London broke all previous records. The pavement scorched Walter's feet through the soles of his shoes as he slowly walked towards Catford Broadway. He was oblivious of heat and discomfort as he pondered deeply about his personal problem. He ignored his surroundings, the plane trees that fringed the roadside, the clanging tramcars and the lightly dressed girls in their flimsy frocks. They failed to register on his mind which was totally submerged in his own private misery.

Since he had begun to bet on the horses, nothing had gone right. The tipsters had let him down time and time again, causing him to repeatedly plunge more heavily to try to recover what he had lost. Walter could see no future beyond the morrow. The auditors would want him to tell them what had become of the two hundred pounds which he knew was missing from his accounts. What could he tell them, other than the truth? And what must happen then?

Instant dismissal was a certainty. At his age he would never be able to get another job without a reference. Anyhow, it was more than probably his employers would prosecute and he would be sent to gaol. Imprisonment? To be locked up in a cell, along with hundreds of debased criminals, slopping out their jerries every morning! How could he ever face Rosie, knowing what was to come? No. No! He simply could not face it. Yet it seemed to him that prison must be the least of his troubles.

His thoughts chased themselves around in his head like rats in a maze. Walter could see no way ahead, until his eyes rested on the open doorway to The Duke of Clarence. The saloon bar was empty at that time of day, and he rapped on the counter until George, the landlord, appeared.

"Hel-lo, Mr Shufflebotham! We don't ever see you in here this time o'day. What'll be your pleasure?"

"A double scotch."

George was a well-trained barman, and concealed his surprise at the unusual request. Obviously, something must be disturbing the old fellow but it was none of his business. George served him his drink in silence then returned to the other bar. Walter Shufflebotham lifted the glass and swallowed half its contents, setting it down with a shudder as the liquor burned his throat. Looking into its amber depths, he saw all at once how ludicrously simple was the solution to his problem. He marvelled that it had taken him so long to perceive how easy out had to be.

No one saw him leave in his haste to carry out his newly-found resolution as Walter emptied the rest of the glass and headed for the doorway inscribed 'Gentlemen'. Several hours later they found Walter sitting in a bolted cubicle. He had severed his carotid artery with an Ever Ready razor blade. Walter Shufflebotham had found the solution to his problem.

Tom Wilson

THE SPIRIT OF GLASGOW NW

I remember my uncle saying
How one morning, walking to work
Down Kelvinside Gardens, carrying
The dullness of his life around him,
Stumbling through the skin of despair
That is synonymous
With the end of love,
He saw a girl,
She walked, not floated,
And the sun shone on her.
Dream dazed he stopped.
She walked (not floated)
past him, but then, turning,
Smiled his youth back to him.
And the despair crinkled a little at the edges
And he knew
It might not always be there.
So that morning, that very morning
that love had left him,
Was the morning that the girl walking
(not floating) in the sun
Smiled.
And was gone.

Letitia Hughes

BODDOM VOE

A round topped black mountain
shone for a minute.
The rainbow colours in it, caught by a rare shaft
of a lighter sky's expression,
Doused at last, by the grey Atlantic
wall of this latest depression.

Force ten, Norwest, for what its worth.
Poly-nuclear-aromatics
From a million years ago,
The very innards of the earth
Are bleeding on the voe.

A kingdom of kelp and broken sands
Of spent and bloodied crags,
With twisted birds and otter pups
that loll like oily rags, in a fidgeting tide.
A smash of Smew, of Golden Eye, of Cormorant and Grebe.
A running sea of greasy words, of carelessness and greed.

Force ten, Norwest, for what its worth.
Toxic Hydro-Carbons
From a million years ago,
The very innards of the earth
Are bleeding on the voe.

A skeleton of steel, and singing hawsers.
Red funnel and a gantry
poke through the heaving foam.
And people from all the causes, come to see
The Brear that came to Shetland, broken and half empty
Bled bleached and beaten twitching on the Boddom shore.

Force ten, Norwest, for what its worth.
Carcinogenic compounds
From a million years ago,
The very innards of the earth
Are bleeding on the voe

Are bleeding on the voe . . .

(The wreck of the Brear at Boddom Voe Shetland   January 1993)

Colin Roberts

BENNIE, SECOND TO NONE

MY DAD'S full name is Bennie Reich. Not Benjamin Reich, nor Ben E. Reich, just plain Bennie Reich. It is simpler that way. Except on forms with three spaces, one for surname, first name and middle name. Once when he filled out such a form not content to leave anything blank, he filled in 'none' for the middle name. We never let him forget the resultant response addressed to Mr. Bennie None Reich. It's one of the few gentle jokes we kids get to tell on him. Most of the time he beats us to the punch line.

He was raised on a North Dakota farm in the middle of the Great Plains during the severe droughts and the depression of the 20s and 30s. It wasn't an easy childhood. Winter winds whistled across the prairie blowing blizzards straight from the Arctic. School was a five mile walk uphill. "Both ways," he would later tell us with a twinkle in his blue eyes. His mother permitted no smoking, no drinking, no swearing, no playing cards, no gambling, and no dancing. The only music allowed was hymn singing - old revivalist tunes like "Rock of Ages" and "Bringing in the Sheaves". At least Grandma succeeded on that one point. To this day it's the only music he enjoys, best sung by someone with his full share of names, Tennessee Ernie Ford. In spite of Grandma's lengthy list of "no's", which he managed to circumvent at some point anyway, he always had the ability to smile. Usually at himself.

Yet there was not much to smile about his service during the war. He spent time in Ireland, England and North Africa. His unit, the Red Bull Division, won medals for seeing more days of combat than any other American division. It was a mortar shell planted in Italy that had his name on it. He lost two fingers on his left hand and got some shrapnel deep into his shoulder and one leg. Bennie spent nearly a year in hospital recovering and doing physical therapy. Despite one leg being shorter than the other due to the injury, he learned how to walk without a limp. When he threw his cane away and married Mom she knew she would spend many hours, years, hemming trouser legs. Every new pair of trousers need to have one leg shortened by one and three quarter inches, a small price to pay, for her. After all, you might say she was partly to blame as they met when she signed him up for the Army.

Bennie's therapy reached a successful conclusion when he regained manual dexterity through making a fine blue cord macrame belt to hold up those lovingly altered trousers, and in the process learned to be at ease with his disabilities. He will tease children by holding up the back of his right hand with the first two fingers folded down into his palm. Giggling, they will ask him to put his other fingers up, or snatch at his hand trying to see and unfold the missing fingers. Then Bennie will hold up his other hand, again with the children viewing it from the front. Still giggling they will ask for the missing fingers to be straightened. But Bennie gets the last laugh - the fingers have truly disappeared.

Just occasionally a disability ceases to be a liability and becomes a positive asset. My whole family are chronically unable to tell left from right. I think it must be genetic. At least with Bennie when he is given directions of that sort one is able to tell him whether it is a two or four finger turn.

After the war he was no longer able to farm for physical reasons so he turned to the next best thing - repairing farm machinery. The Army assisted by sending him on a mechanics course. Gackle Brothers General Store, furniture, grains bought and sold, hardware, cars, funerals, cattle auctions, and tractors, gave him a job. He repaired all those hard-worked tractors of his neighbours. As a mechanic he knew his work was solidly reliable and stood behind every repair he did. "Except one," he told us, "a muck spreader."

In 1951 he moved to the big city, St. Paul, in the neighbouring state of Minnesota. Passing the test for Postal Employees he started working on the railway mail where he rode the overnight train sorting letters as the train travelled from St. Paul to Chicago, and then back. During the days between trips to Chicago (three days on the road, four days off) he would teach us kids how to play those card games forbidden in his childhood - pinochle, cribbage, Black Jack, a little poker. Bets were made with matchsticks or bottle caps. He always won those games, except when his sense of good parenting got the better of him and he'd let us win.

He'd light his pipe, crack open a salted-in-the-shell peanut and we'd all have a terrific afternoon. Only Mom would mutter to herself about what heathens we were becoming and finally say to us "Don't you tell Grandma about this." I don't know why our card playing upset her so much. Her father used to run illegal liquor during prohibition. Got thrown into jail too, for running wine from California, but that's another story.

But the time of the trains turned to the time of the planes. Bennie, still with the Post Office, began sorting letters at the airport. Although this meant more regular hours, the familiar camaraderie of the rails was lost. During this period Bennie started dreaming out loud. For a year at a time he would periodically refer to "When we move to Australia..." Another year the refrain was "When we move to Colorado and become sheep herders.." Slowly the dreams crept closer to home. "When we move to Wisconsin and buy a farm.." Then when my brother was 13 it was "When we enter the St. Paul to Winnipeg snowmobile race.."

That one made us all sit up. Snowmobiles were not new to Minnesotans, but they were to my father and brother. Neither had ever been on one. Undaunted, they set off to the dealers showrooms and returned home with glossy brochures and an application form for the 500 mile race. They had it all planned, Bennie with his mechanical skills would look after the machine, my brother would drive the gruelling, semi-professional race while Mom and I would wait at the mid and endpoints with steaming mugs of cocoa. We had to talk a whole lot faster than the snowmobile salesman, but we managed to talk them out of it.

The Post Office began to make some very attractive offers to entice people to retire early rather than face redundancy in the mid 1970's. As the months turned over the offers got better and Mom's worries became bigger. She liked having her days to herself. Bennie had no hobbies, never read anything but the daily paper and the Readers Digest (and that is always left in the toilet), so what would he do all day?

We tried to think up time absorbing hobbies: stamp collecting (he could still go down to visit his buddies at the post office, we thought it was ideal). "I worked with stamps all my life, I don't need to keep on doing it." Bee keeping (not difficult, and we could eat the honey). "Can't stand insects." How about redoing the garden, making it really special? "Our place is too shady, plants don't take there." In exasperation we blurted out, "But what are you going to do?" He calmly replied "If I wanted to do something I'd keep on working."

And that is just what he did in June 1978. Nothing. It drove Mom crazy. It drove us crazy. He was like a three year old, always at your elbow wanting to help, to know what you were doing, and why were you doing it this way? But then equilibrium set in. He answered an advertisement in the paper to volunteer at the local retirement home to play cribbage with some of the men. He joined his old railway mail buddies at the Rod and Gun Club. He joined the honour guard at the Veteran's cemetery to help bury the dead with dignity. He joined the Disabled American Veterans. He helped out at church. He joined the American Legion. Soon he was so busy Mom had to join the women's affiliations of his new clubs in order to see him some days.

Although he'd always had a vegetable garden, almost a necessity with us five children and a postman's salary, it was never an obsession or even an interest. It was something that had to be done, like mowing the lawn. Then one summer my brother, wanting to play tennis, couldn't find his yellow tennis balls. It turned out Bennie had borrowed them to put in the garden as "role models" for his cucumbers (I think he had been reading one too many articles from his toilet library). We thought he'd gone past his sell by date until lunch one day a few weeks later when he brought in his first harvest: two round, yellow cucumbers exactly the size of the tennis balls. Bennie's only comment was to my brother, "Can I borrow your basketball for the pumpkin patch?"

Bennie and Mom also began to travel more extensively around America. But I was living and working in Africa, and I wanted them to visit there. I explained that just reading about it or seeing the places on television isn't good enough, and how enlightening travel can be. I knew money was no longer such a problem without us five kids at home any more. But I always received the same answer, a flat no. Then suddenly they agreed to meet me halfway, in Britain, where they could at least speak the language or so they thought, they hadn't reckoned on Dave, my soon-to-be husband's Devon accent).

Although Bennie had been here briefly in the war he didn't know where, as they had removed all the signposts. Going around the country Mom would exclaim how quaint and delightful it was, while Bennie would only offer "Yep, just like when I was here in the war. Nothing has changed."

London confused him a bit, but not without reason. Dave was playing the true host, taking us all sightseeing by car, although he himself had only used the underground on his previous visits. Consequently navigation and traffic became quite hair-raising. It didn't help either that my directions, given with my nose in the A-Z, were of the "Turn left here. No, your other left" variety, (a consequence of the Reich inability to differentiate left and right). In the end Dave discovered that no matter where we were starting from or going to, the easiest route was to return to Trafalgar Square, go around it two or three times until we spotted a sign for the next stop on our tour. About the fourth time that day as we, once again circled Trafalgar, Bennie looked up at Nelson's statue and asked "What happened to his horse? This morning we went around he was on a horse. What have they done with it?"

Now into his seventies he feels able to indulge, if only occasionally, in that long ago forbidden, and therefore much longed for real gambling. When visiting my sister in California among his list of "must-do's" such as playing with the grandkids and fixing her leaky toilet - she too keeps her copy of the Readers' Digest there - is one very special day on his own. He removes his wallet and all his credit cards, puts $100 in his pocket (saved for just this occasion) and climbs on the freebie bus to Lake Tahoe, Nevada where gambling is legal. No longer confined to matchsticks or bottle caps he plays the casino games with abandon. He lingers over the Black Jack tables, pumps coins into the one armed bandits, enjoying the losing as well as the winning. Once inside there are no clocks, and no windows. It is perpetual gambling time. He has many years to make up for, and only $100 to do it with. Playing until his money runs out, he then boards the bus and returns to the grandkids, content until the next visit.

Except once. That time, try as he did, he just kept on winning. The more he played, the more he won. Tiredness overcame excitement. He finally boarded the bus home with more than $100 and an additional 50 silver dollars weighing down his pockets. I can prove it. He divided those silver dollars among us kids. And I still have all 10 of mine.

Lori M. Reich

FALLEN SWIFT, ASHFORD

Screaming Ariel, curved blade
Slicing the sky, hits a high wire
Tumbles on Denmark Road
The arc and angle of its wing at odds
And unmatched to its partner -
It is broken. Hood the head
With Kleenex tissue
To still the panick'd claws.
Hide in a Tesco's bag
The throbbing body. Check
The watchful lustrous eyes
That close...and open.. close,
Patient with pain.
Scan Yellow Pages
Searching for saviours.
Five squat ticks run out
Run from the host so suddenly grounded
Scutter around in the plastic bag
An ugly freight, a summary unloading,
Unscheduled stop, a change
Of continent, confounded.

Pat McNeill

Sometimes, in the morning I'll remember,
and the taste is still there
of your skin.
Hung over from you.
I start the day slowly,
wandering through the ritual,
blaming the night for becoming almost dust
almost dust;
for you became inside me
fused,
and each part mutated
so you, am I
I taste you,
such mornings.

By lunchtime
all hope of you is gone,
and the afternoon holds little.
At Four you come, unexpectedly,
but stay hardly at all.
You seem distrait,
as if you have lost something.

I have your taste,
it is here.

Letitia Hughes

WAVING TO STRANGERS

THERE WOULD be no visitors today. She had been very careful and just a little unkind in preserving her privacy.

'I am sorry. Yes, it would have been nice. But there it is you see I've already made plans.'

'Tomorrow? Oh, what a shame, if only I'd known sooner. Perhaps another time? Of course I will. You must give me a ring and let me know.'

The third time the telephone rang she had almost weakened.

'Well... I'm not sure. I mean I'm not sure what's happening yet. Well I'll probably know this evening' and then she had tightened her resolve. 'It wouldn't be fair really, changing plans at the last minute and it would be such a long way for you to come and then find....' she didn't have to finish the sentence 'Oh, well, good, if you can do that instead... yes... enjoy yourself then, give them my love.'

She had managed it without telling an actual lie but if called upon to tell the truth what could she have said?

'What exactly are you doing tomorrow, Jennie, that is so important that it means more to you than a visit from your sister?'

There would have been no reply to that direct question because tomorrow she was doing nothing but what made it so important was that she was doing it all by herself.

There would come a day, she knew, when the telephone wouldn't ring and perhaps she would want it to. She just needed the space. A strange modern phrase that, but so descriptive. She needed to know that the space stretched out in all directions, to the sky, to the horizon. She wanted to be sealed in a huge space bubble.

The early morning August sun rose in the sky behind the branches of the tall slender silver birch trees which bordered the garden and shaded the lawn, but shone across the top of the laburnum directly onto the side of the house where Jennie sat on the step. She felt the shaft of sunlight soak into her body. It touched her like a magic wand.

'I am your fairy godmother and you shall go to the Ball'.

Jennie smiled and relaxed even further into the softness of the pillows placed in the corner of the open doorway. She fingered the silky material of her skirt, it had always been a favourite, the pattern somehow oriental, the colours a mixture of blending blues and turquoise, a splash of red and black. Cut short now to above her knees it was still a joy to wear. Full length, pencil slim, worn with a black silk blouse it had been sensational. Not another one like it in the whole world. That was the joy of creation. And that was how Jennie felt about herself. And on her own, today, that was how she could be. Not the Jennie people thought she was, or the Jennie they thought she should be, or the Jennie they hoped she might become, the Jennie that she was - not another one like her in the whole world. Why did people feel uncomfortable if they couldn't put you in a group?

'I don't understand you, Jennie, I don't understand you at all.'

What they meant was,

'You're not behaving as I think you should - you're not completing the pattern.'

Life was a pattern - one vast tapestry with each action a movement through the canvas and Jennie was going to choose her own colours, her own stitches, and her own thread. She was going to complete it slowly and quietly so that when she came to the last final knot she would remember every stitch, every shade, nothing would be left out and the completed picture would be Jennie.

She eased the skirt up, making it even shorter, and stretched her legs out. Unbuttoning her blouse she slipped it off and the heat of the sun touched the newly exposed skin of her bare breasts almost, she felt, like the hands of a lover, gentle and exploring. Jennie had known gentle and exploring lovers but none of them had known Jennie.

The sun had risen now above the trees and shone upon the whole of the garden. The colours of the flowers were vivid against the greens of the leaves, each petal daubed with brilliant paint, as though an artist's brush had flicked across the flower bed and yet achieved such a perfection of blending, such a balance of contrasts, such a variety of patterns that no accident could have achieved such perfection. Peacock butterflies were feeding on the white buddleia and bees buzzed around and nosed their way, gentle and exploring, into the deep recesses of bugle shaped flowers.

One fearless peacock flew over to Jennie and settled on the white pages of her book.

'Ah, an intellectual butterfly' thought Jennie, and carefully studied the tiny head and body which was the real insect.

'We don't always notice the real you, do we. There you are waving those beautiful fragile wings around, pretending to have such big soulful eyes when all the time there you are hidden underneath. How are we to know that you like reading books?'

She looked carefully at the little creature as it waved its slender antennae and flicked its tongue. She would have liked to stroke its tiny head but knew that such close contact was not allowed and, as if aware of staying in one place too long, the beautiful wings came together softly and then opened and lifted the creature soundlessly into the air.

'I can understand your desire for privacy with such a naked vulnerable body and yet you want to be noticed and then when you wave those beautiful wings you're misunderstood.'

Jennie raised her head, her hand above her eyes to shade them from the light as she heard a steady droning and there, in the sky, appearing directly above her head was what looked like a giant moth. Jennie tipped her head sideways to get a better view. It was an amazing sight and the sheer wonder of it made Jennie laugh. What an amazing way to travel! What a wonderful view there must be for whoever was flying the craft. Childlike with excitement Jennie leapt up from the step and stood on the open lawn. Raising her arm in the air she waved. From below there was no way of knowing whether the person in control of the craft could see her or not. Jennie waved anyway. If they couldn't see her then it wouldn't matter that she was behaving like a child and if they could, well, what kind an adult strapped himself to wings and flew? Perhaps it was Icarus trying once again to find a balance between flying high and not getting your wings burned. She watched the wings disappear over the tops of the trees and turned back to her book.

She had just got herself in a comfortable position when she became aware of a strengthening of the droning and looking up again saw that the great wings had changed course and were flying back towards her. She could hardly believe it. Hand on mouth she looked up into the sky, and then down at her bare skin, aware only now of her nakedness, and laughing out loud she stretched both arms into the air and waved. She felt she was being courted and, charmed by the reckless behaviour of her suitor, she was in love. And yet was she in love with the wings or the real person? Or were the wings part of the real person? Detached from the wings Icarus fell into the sea and was drowned. She watched and waved as the stranger circled once above her head and then moved off again away from her over the trees. She stood watching until there was only empty sky and the droning engine faded.

Jennie looked at the garden full to overflowing with colour, looked at the peacock butterflies on the buddleia and stretching her arms out she danced slowly across the lawn, moving in circles, now dipping her head and stretching her arms out now behind her, now lifting her head and waving her arms in front like antennae, the colours on her skirt matching with the bright petals of the flowers, her brown body slender and alive with movement.

Marjorie Burge

IN THANKS FOR JOCELYN'S POTTERY

Jossy's bowls are big as breasts
Smooth inside like thrushes' nests
Brown as Scottish burns in spate,
Round their warmth my two hands meet.
Treasures! When at last you crack
How to plastic wares go back?

Bowls are meant for wear and tear
Breakage is their mortal lot,
Future fellows digging here
And finding shards from Jossy's pot
Will rate our era not as pigs
With paper plates and styro mugs,
But on their evidence will judge
Ours was the truly Golden Age.

Pat McNeill

WINTER ORCHARDS SEEN FROM THE TRAIN

Ivory-wooled the sheep move
Among blanched grasses
All identical animals under the orchards'
Winter scribble of branches.
A pale amber sun from a bone-coloured sky
Flicks on the flints in far, bleaching fields.
All the green is gone and the burning blues
Of June. Only in boughs here and there
A missed apple hangs like a lantern
Left over from summer's party
Red and forgotten.

Pat McNeill

THE FACELESS SQUARE

THE CROSS channel ferry was strangely empty but I was not at all surprised. If I had had any sense, I would not be on it either. The weather report in the last hour was forecasting force nine gales in the English Channel, and I could see huge breakers crashing over the harbour wall.

I hurriedly chewed my "Sea-Leg' tablets only five minutes before sailing, and washed them down with a large brandy, pushing to the back of my mind that drugs and alcohol do not mix.

Sitting opposite me was a member of the ship's crew, a middle-aged lady with grey-streaked hair and a pleasant smile. She was manageress of the gift shop on the deck below and was now off duty.

"How was the crossing?" I asked apprehensively.
"A little choppy" she replied.
"I'll bet it was choppy!" I thought.

A male steward appeared in a black, pinstriped suit, which was shiny at the knees, carrying paper bags for the queasy amongst us. He was a chatterbox and rattled on about the ship being back from its latest re-fit. He pointed out the brand new, colourful carpets and tables; then, as an afterthought, mentioned that it was very rough out there in the middle of the channel, and offered me a bag.

"Some people just can't handle it" was his parting shot.

I turned my back on the porthole and tried to make myself comfortable, closing my eyes and pretending that I was on dry land, sitting in a bus. As we sailed out of the harbour, leaving the white cliffs of Dover behind us, the ferry lurched and shuddered as we hit a monstrous wave.

"It will take more than the scheduled two hours, at this rate" I thought.

This was the first time that I had made the crossing alone, but I was not concerned, as my boyfriend, Tom, would be there to meet me. He had given me very clear and precise instructions that he would meet me in the covered walk-way, especially built for foot passengers.

It was a very rough crossing, and I felt desperately ill, not being a good sailor. Waves of nausea swept over me and icy, cold beads of sweat ran in rivulets down my spine. I thought that the journey would never end, and I prayed to die.

Then the shout came,

"Harbour Stations!"

I felt such a great sense of relief, knowing that it would only be ten minutes before docking and getting off the boat. Saying goodbye to the lady from the gift-shop, I made my way down to the next deck, following the passengers down the ramp and on to the quayside.

Three teenage boys were leading the way, followed by a young couple with a babe in arms; then there was a middle-aged couple and myself. I just could not seem to keep up with them, and they got further and further ahead of me, until they disappeared completely from sight. I stood still, trying not to panic, which was not easy as I have no sense of direction. Even if it had been daylight and the sun had been shining, I would not have known where I was.

The pigskin week-end case was quite heavy and had made my fingers go numb. The high-fashion boots that I had bought especially for the occasion were pinching my little toe and were certainly never meant for hiking abroad. I could see orange lights in the distance and thought that this must be the customs, so picking up my bag I started walking again.

The wind had now dropped, and a sea-mist was creeping stealthily forward, making everything seem unreal. The dock area was very grey and bleak; huge soot covered buildings dominated the skyline and I felt so alone and vulnerable. I hurried on towards the orange lights, stumbling over what appeared to be old tram lines; then I realised that I was between sleepers.

"What if a train comes along?"

The whole place stank of exhaust fumes mixed with fish.

"Of course, this town is famous for its fish. I'm sure that I passed that viaduct half an hour ago."

I was becoming quite out of breath and the orange lights seemed to be even further away. It was no use; I would have to rest and try to get my bearings. There was nowhere to sit and a distinct lack of signs.

"It is ridiculous! How can I be walking along in a big European Port without being asked for my papers?"

"Where is everyone? Where are the dock workers? Come out, come out, wherever you are. I have nothing to declare except one bottle of whisky, which I will drink on the spot if challenged."

"Please come and find me, please!" I cried out.

A bark, followed by a hair-raising howl, shattered the silence of the night and I was rooted to the ground. I trembled with fear, and wondered what strange animal could be in such despair. It was almost an anti-climax when a poor, bedraggled, black and white mongrel dog appeared from the direction of an old warehouse, wagging his tail.

"Oh no" I said. I was an animal lover but there was no chance of me patting his head. He could be rabid.

He ran towards me, wagging his tail and drooling at the mouth, obviously pleased to see me. The feeling was not mutual. He sat at my feet and raised his front paws in a begging position; the appeal in his eyes could not be ignored, so resting my case on the ground, I stooped down, scratching him behind his right ear.

Well, I supposed it would be all right - after all, he is supposed to be man's best friend. I rummaged in my handbag and found some chocolate, which he gulped down with one large swallow, looking up for more. Perhaps he would lead me out of this nightmare; it was worth a try.

The two of us set off, down the road together, he bounding on ahead, looking back all the time to see if I was following him. After some time he stopped at what appeared to be an old aircraft hangar and with an excited bark, disappeared inside. I followed more cautiously, not entirely happy with the situation, just in time to see him bound away into a corner behind some old packing cases.

"This is ridiculous. I must have been mad to follow him into this desolate place." My thoughts were running wild.

Feeling in my pocket for a small torch, I turned to leave, despairing of ever getting to my destination, when something furry brushed my leg. I went rigid, stifled a scream, and stabbed the torch downwards into the blackness. I breathed again when I saw three muling, black and white puppies playing with my feet.

This was getting me nowhere, so I hurried away, unwilling to take on the whole family.

The fog was thinning out, although I could still hear the foghorns out at sea, wailing their dismal lament. Looming up, out of the mist, were clusters of tall, grey pillars, reaching skywards at least twenty metres high. Perched across each one was what looked like an eighteenth century railway carriage, the blinds drawn with pillars of light peeping through the cracks, forming a sort of square. I looked up bewildered.

"Was this the covered walk-way for foot passengers at last¦" It did not seem to lead anywhere.

I hurried along, searching desperately for the entrance.

"I'm sure that I passed that sign, advertising cigars, years ago."

Suddenly, to the left of the sign, I noticed some dilapidated steps built out of yellow house bricks, leading upwards towards the carriages. Struggling up the steps, with my cases in both hands, I came to a glass panelled door, with no visible signs of entry. Fortunately, it had been vandalised, and one huge pane was missing, so it was a simple job to duck under the metal bar and into the walkway.......

Relief flooded through me. At last I had found the rendezvous, although I knew that I was very late. I started running through the winding corridors, my heart beating madly. Every corridor looked the same - steel blue aluminium walls, fluted like fences. The ceilings were black and shiny with subdued fluorescent lighting suspended on black chains. There did not appear to be any other travellers. All I could hear were my own footsteps. I was about to despair when I came across a metal barrier.

"Ah," I thought "this must be the customs."

Putting my case on the ground I felt in my handbag for my passport, but the barrier was unmanned. I heaved the barriers apart with maniacal strength, and took a few venturesome steps beyond, but it was no use. I had come to a dead end. I was obviously walking in the wrong direction and would have to re-trace my steps.

By now, I was completely disorientated and had lost all sense of time. It was becoming a great effort to drag myself along. Dear dear Tom. He was somewhere in this great architectural masterpiece looking for me. I kept going forward automatically, like a punch drunk, not knowing when to give up. Then I heard a humming noise in the distance like the sound of whirring blades from a helicopter. I hurried towards the sound, filled with fresh hope, and came upon an escalator which, as I got nearer, started moving downwards, joining a tarmacadam road.

"This is an improvement. It must lead somewhere." I could see more orange lights and signs of activity as I hurried along the road. A short, stocky man came towards me, hand raised.

"Reisepass bitte."

"Ah. Trying to catch me out," I thought, "I know enough words to get by in France.

"Reisepass bitte. Schnell, schnell."

Hold on a minute. That's German, not French," I said.

I flourished my passport in front of his face but he only gave it a cursory glance and said in broken English.

"Hurry please, Miss, boat for England leave now."

"But I have just come from England," I replied, bewildered. He looked at me wonderingly, then speaking very slowly, he said,

"You must be mistaken, Miss. There is no boat from Dover for one week. Seamen's strike."

Waves of nausea swept over me and I knew I was going to be sick. I felt a cool hand on my forehead and a rustle of paper, accompanied by a voice coming from a long distance.

"Come on now, buck up, we will be docking in five minutes, Harbour Stations have been called."

I sat bolt upright in my seat, reaching for the paper bag, but it was too late. I was sick all over the nice, red carpet. Looking up into the face of the gift shop lady, I felt so ashamed.

"Don't worry. It can't be helped," she said.

"I don't understand," I said.

"You were the lucky one sleeping all the way," she said with wry humour. "It was the worst crossing I have ever experienced in my ten years of service.

The boat was blessedly still now, having docked and passengers were hurrying to disembark. I said goodbye to the gift shop lady, following the other passengers heading for the overhead gantry, making sure that I kept up this time. As I came down the steps and on to the dockside, I heard a shout.

"Liz, Liz, over here!"

It was my dear Tom. I flew into his arms, kissing and hugging him as if there was no tomorrow. He was a little surprised by my behaviour, as I was not usually this demonstrative in public.

"You poor old thing, it must have been a terrible crossing."

"Not too bad," I murmured, "Although I'm glad you met me off the boat."

"Well, I thought it the best thing to do, knowing your sense of direction, and the covered walk-way isn't too easy to find, especially in the dark."

I laughed, saying, "You have no faith in me."

We walked away from the ship, following the other passengers along a railway track towards some orange lights in the distance. I kept tight hold of his hand, delighting in his closeness.

A black and white mongrel dog ran towards me, jumping up and splashing my coat with his muddy paws.

"Don't touch it, it may be rabid," Tom said, shifting him with the toe of his shoe.

Passing an advertisement for cigars, we then turned left and there were the dilapidated yellow brick steps. I stopped, turning to Tom.

"Where are you taking me?" I asked nervously.

"Don't look so worried. I know a short cut which will save us lots of time" he replied.

"No, Tom. I'm not going up there." I said firmly.

"But Liz, it's quicker this way," he replied.

I had this deep sense of foreboding, and my whole body was screaming out that something was wrong.

"I would rather follow the others, Tom."

"Come on, Liz," he said more gently, "I'm dying for a drink and there's a bar in the walkway."

Reluctantly, and against my better judgment, I followed him up the yellow brick steps, under the metal bar, and into the walkway.

It was very hot and crowded with people, pushing and shoving, eager to get away.

The full-throated scream when it came was shrill and relentless. People turned to stare, and Tom made a grab for me, but I backed away from him and ran screaming at the top of my voice along the corridors that I knew so well. I came upon the steel barrier, and collapsed in a heap, moaning.

The foghorns were wailing their distress out at sea, and banks of rolling fog were closing fast.....

Come quickly......

Freda Evans

THE TRAMP'S SONG

A tramp I am, a tramp indeed,
A'tramping through the countryside,
With dirty wellies, shabby clothes,
Compass and map my only guide.
A gipsy I would seem, to be,
Dusty, travel tired, that's me.

But friend, I have some priceless gifts
Bestowed on me by country ways.
A fresh, free air I breathe within.
I wander as I will for days.
I have a freedom of the soul
Free from conformity and role.

I see the growth of flowers, of plants,
Of birds and animals - shy of man.
The wider heavens are at my glance.
I know the secret place of Pan.
All God's great gifts of Nature rare
Are to my eyes and mind laid bare.

No place, position, status great
Can with this freedom fine compare
No money, time, possessions, style
Can take the place of country fair.
Where all His glorious works abound
The love of God wraps me around.

We cannot buy His bounteous gifts,
Thus are His just ways seen abroad.
To all who wish and will to take,
Gives so generously our Lord.
I own the land on which I roam
More than the owner in his home.

Violet Sime

THE GREEN TICKET

RICHARD COULDN'T contain himself. "Yeow!" he yelled, and smoothed the tele-letter across the glass worktop holding it flat with the tips of his fingers.

The lottery ticket number was embossed across the letterhead just above the word 'congratulations', and the smarmy happy language of the letter made him grin with satisfaction.

"I've won, I've won, and a family ticket at that!" His mind worked overtime.

"If I wanted to sell this it would raise a million I'd bet. But who'd want to, yeah who'd want to. Oh boy, just wait until I tell the wife, she'll go mad ... just mad, I know she will. Huh, she'll have all the neighbours eating out of her hands ..... Mmm! that's if we tell them. Perhaps it would be better to keep mum about it, I mean, I heard of one bloke having his stolen, and there was that other fella who sold his, and his wife and family were so mad they all up't and left him."

"Gosh..." he looked once more at the ticket with its colourful watermark and lovely print. 'Family Ticket' that's what it said. So really, it was theirs as much as his. Mind you he'd applied for it all those years ago. All those years of watching for the number of the draw on the resultex, huh, how they all called him a bore, and tut-tutted at him for driving them to their own screens those evenings.

"Ahh.. ah! I'll be king now though. I have it here in my hand. Worth a small fortune and a chance of a lifetime."

Walking to the door Richard pressed the access button, went through into the solar store and gazed happily upwards as the dark green UV hood peeled slowly backwards with a slight humming of the motors.

Pivoting in his chair he then punched the start button, and gave it his voice pattern, saying 'Richard' in a false deliberate way.

He always hoped he would some day beat the logic of the computer but after two or three seconds it answered in a monotone squeak that never failed to make him smile... "Ultra violet angle calculated at sixty two degrees... exposure to radiation set for seven minutes... click." His chair tilted on auto and the warm sun tingled his cheeks.....

Mmmm! that was nice... a whole seven minutes of sunshine to think about the 'big one...' The big day out... the big event! Yippee!

Richard heard the docking gates rattle just as he'd finished in the solar store and happy as he was he couldn't resist cursing women pilots.

"You'll knock the blooming docking handles off it you don't park more carefully, darling."

His wife looked at him hard, trying to judge his mood. She knew the last time she'd pranged the docking handles they all had to sleep in their helmets whilst they mended the air lock as well.

"Sorry darling... hey, you've had too much sun, look at your nose."

He felt the end of his nose instinctively.

"No I haven't... it's not possible anyway."

"Well you've been in there though haven't you?"

"True, true, I've nearly had my quota for the month. Still I was feeling happy, a bit of good news you see."

"News, what news?"

He held up the ticket and like everything else it took on the green glow of the room.

"Let me see," she said, but his wife couldn't quite see, so made to snatch for the ticket and Richard pulled it away playfully.

"Guess," he shouted. "Just guess!"

No need to," she answered straining to see the print. "It's! Yes, it's the lottery! No, you wouldn't kid me..."

She could see from the light in his eyes it was true.

"Yeeeow!!" She jumped with delight.. Yeeow!! Wonderful. I just must speak to Jennifer."

"W...Wait!" Richard put his hand over the inter-mike. "Is that wise?"

"Why ever not?" she replied.

"Well... er.. the begging letters.. er.. and remember that couple who were robbed. Don't you think we ought to keep it quiet?"

He could see now he'd stolen half of his wife's pleasure. To be the envy of everyone didn't come too often these days and his heart softened.

"Oh, alright then," he grinned "But you'll have to sleep with it in your bra for a couple of weeks, okay?"

When the children came home they too were delirious at the news and were quick to swamp the air, telling all their friends until the whole environ was alive with the detail of their good fortune.

Richard's drinking partner, Joe Blake, was the first one to call, his voice crackling through the ether.
"Hey Richard you lucky old devil. Just thought I'd give you a shout to say congratulations.. you know I remember my great great grandfather telling me about when those things were quite the thing around here... and .."
"You knew your great great grandfather?" interrupted Richard.
"Well you know he lived to a very great age did my ..."
"Oh come on... really Joe."
"Well, okay, but I remember hearing talk of how lovely they were and now you're actually going to see one. And you know, we have one of those encapsulated keep safe things, and they're collectors items now. It's a real nice one, all red and yellow with five points... not one of the brown filigree'd one's. Not many people have seen one, never mind have one. He used to say they were as common as yeast extract you know, and we all used to laugh cos' he still ate the stuff."
"Who did?" interrupted Richard.
"Well, my great great grandfather of course."
"Really, Joe... Anyway, thanks for your good wishes. Our ticket is for a week on Thursday so I'll tell you all about it over a drink on the Friday, okay?"
"Well that's a good idea Richard, thanks, but hey, don't forget, if any of you get sick, well er .. I mean any of us would just love to fill in er..."
"Yeah, yeah, I've got your drift but, we'll all go even if we're dying, don't worry. Bye Joe."

Richard put his hand over the transmit shield and looked at his wife, saying "What a damned cheek!"
She nodded understandingly.
"His bloody great great grandfather indeed!"
His wife smiled at him again.
"It's possible darling."
"Bloody unlikely though, and as for those encapsulated keepsakes,

I don't ever remember seeing one when we've been to their place do you?'

"Can't say I've noticed, darling, but then it's probably kept in the safe, wouldn't you say?"

"Mmm maybe... Anyway, we're' going to see the real thing. The biggest attraction this country has to offer, so stuff Joe, and his great great grandfather. There's people would give a year's wages to have our ticket, so hang on to it tight, alright darling?"

His wife put her hand to her bra, then looked self-consciously at the children.

"It's safe with me," she said.

When Thursday came, Richard and his family took the early land craft to the international assembly station where they bought four seats on the power tube to the World Exhibition Centre full of expectation and excitement. Food and wine were included. Then with a capacity crowd of four hundred thousand other lucky prize winners, they sat down to view the most spectacular sight on earth.

There, floodlit in pale green and gold and red, pampered in a fine falling mist of spray, and played iridescently under delicate laser beams, it stood in all its glory. Twisting finely at every angle in all the colours of brown with clingy grey and lime green lichens, and every collecting and condensing drop from that fine mist gathering in its great bulk to make a sound equal only to the applause of those who sat amazed at this impossible beauty.

"That" whispered Richard to his wide eyed family "Is the world's last remaining tree."

Colin Roberts